PIANO TUNES
FOR CHILDREN

Anthony Marks

Edited by Jenny Tyler
Designed by Doriana Berkovic

Illustrated by Simone Abel
and Kim Blundell

Music selected, arranged and edited by Anthony Marks
New compositions by Anthony Marks
Piano advisor: John York
Music setting: Andrew Jones
Managing designer: Russell Punter

About this book

You will already know some of these tunes, though others might be less familiar. Three of them were written specially for this book. If you have a computer, you can listen to all the tunes on the Usborne Quicklinks Website to hear how they go. Just go to **www.usborne-quicklinks.com** and enter the keywords "piano tunes", then follow the simple instructions.

At the top of every piece there is a picture in a circle. Each of these has a sticker to match in the middle of the book. Use these to show that you have learned the piece. There are star stickers too, to use if you or your teacher think you play a piece very well.

Contents

Nkosi sikelel iAfrika

The English title of this tune is "Lord bless Africa". It was written in 1897 by Enoch Sontonga, and is now the national anthem of South Africa.

Majestically ♩ = 92

Throughout this book you will find suggestions for dynamics (how loud or quiet to play), as well as markings that tell you how fast or slow the music should be. Use these as a guide when you are learning the pieces, but remember that they are only suggestions.

Once you know the music, try it faster or slower, or with different dynamics. Compare different versions and decide which you like best. When you find a version you like, remember it for next time you play the tune. Deciding on speed and dynamics is part of your skill as a player.

This train is bound for glory

Nobody knows who wrote this tune, or the one opposite. They are both American and were probably first sung in the 19th century.

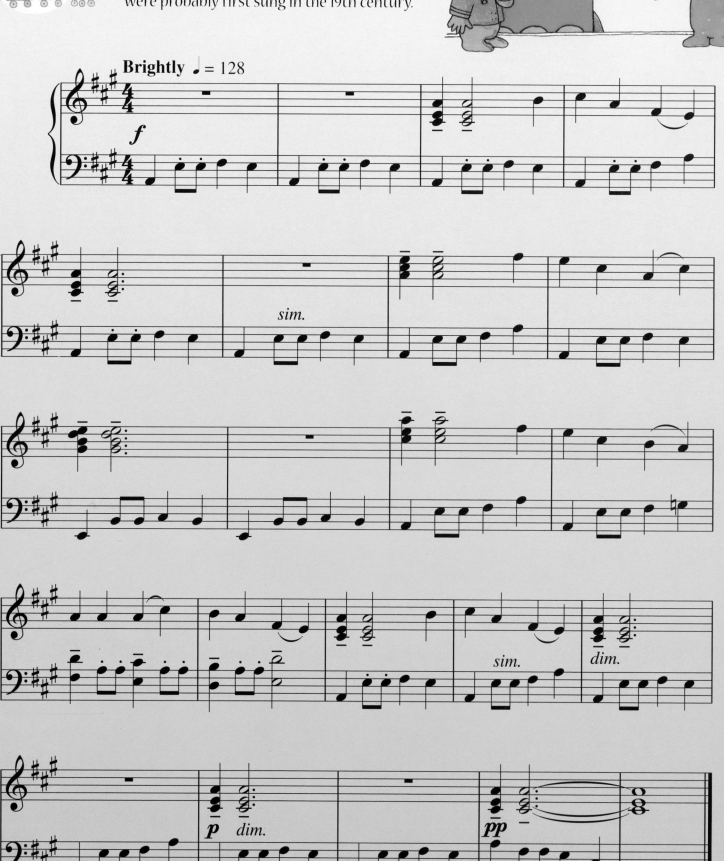

Will the circle be unbroken?

Both these tunes are religious songs, and were probably first sung by slaves or poor farmers in the southern USA.

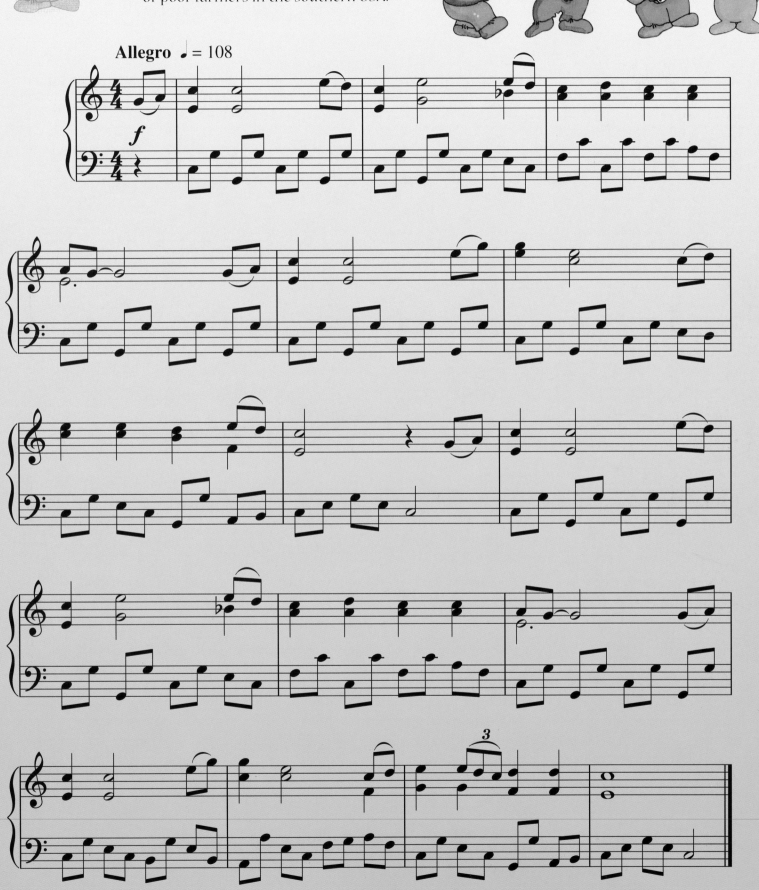

Simple gifts

Joseph Brackett, a member of an
American religious group called the
Shakers, wrote this tune in 1848.

Up in the air

This piece was written specially for this book. Follow the accidentals carefully - and watch out for the 4/4 bar.

Les moissonneurs

The French composer François Couperin wrote this piece in 1716, for an old keyboard instrument called a harpsichord. The title means "The harvesters".

D.C. al Fine

Both these pieces are about harvesting. People used to sing while gathering crops because the rhythm of the music made the work easier.

Can you find several pieces that are based on the same idea, or in the same style, or from the same country, or by the same composer? You could play them together in a concert.

Song of the reapers

The German composer Schumann
wrote this in 1848. It is one of a group
of pieces for young people called
"Album for the young".

Polonaise

This piece and the one opposite were written by J. S. Bach, a German composer who lived from 1685 to 1750.

Andante ♩ = 72

A polonaise is an old dance from Poland with slow, elegant steps. Try to imagine this when you play the music to help you feel the rhythm. Moving to music helps you understand it. Once you know a piece, sing it out loud or in your head. Invent hand movements or steps to match it.

What kind of gestures would you use for a slow, smooth piece? Are they the same as the ones you use for a fast, lively tune?

Musette

This tune has a continuous left-hand note called a drone. It imitates an old instrument called a musette, which is a kind of bagpipe.

Moderato ♩ = 88

It was a lover and his lass

The English composer Thomas Morley wrote this tune. It was published in 1600, and was also used in Shakespeare's play "As you like it".

The sailor woman

Nobody knows who wrote this tune. It
was first published in the 17th century
in France, but it is much older than that.

Jenny pluck pears

This piece and the one opposite are
tunes to old English dances. They were
first published in 1651 in a book called
"The Dancing Master".

Delicately   ♩. = 72

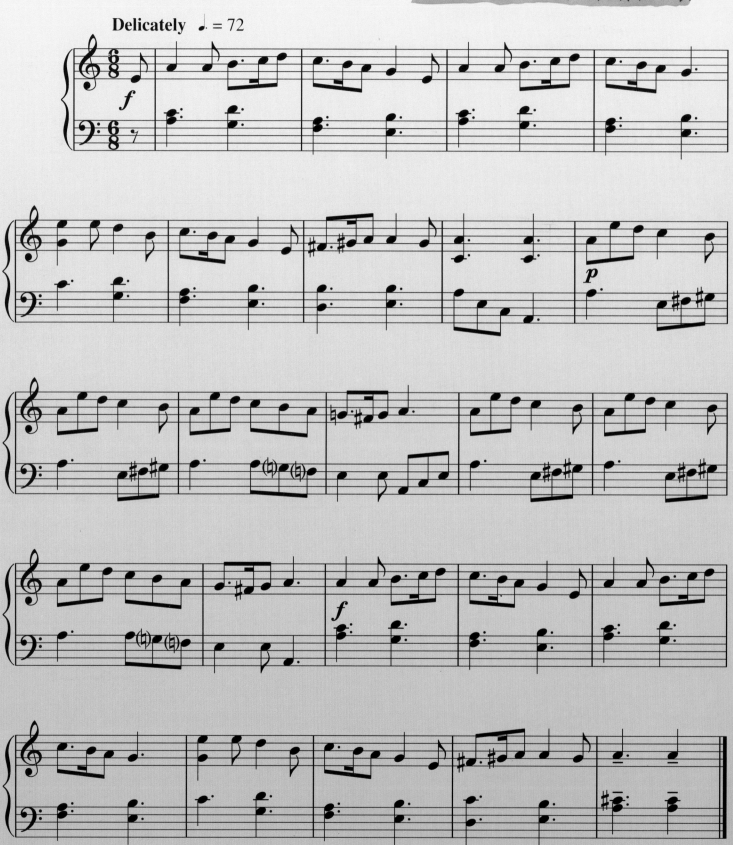

Gathering peascods

"The Dancing Master" contains the tunes and steps for hundreds of country dances. It was published by John Playford, a musician and bookseller who lived in London.

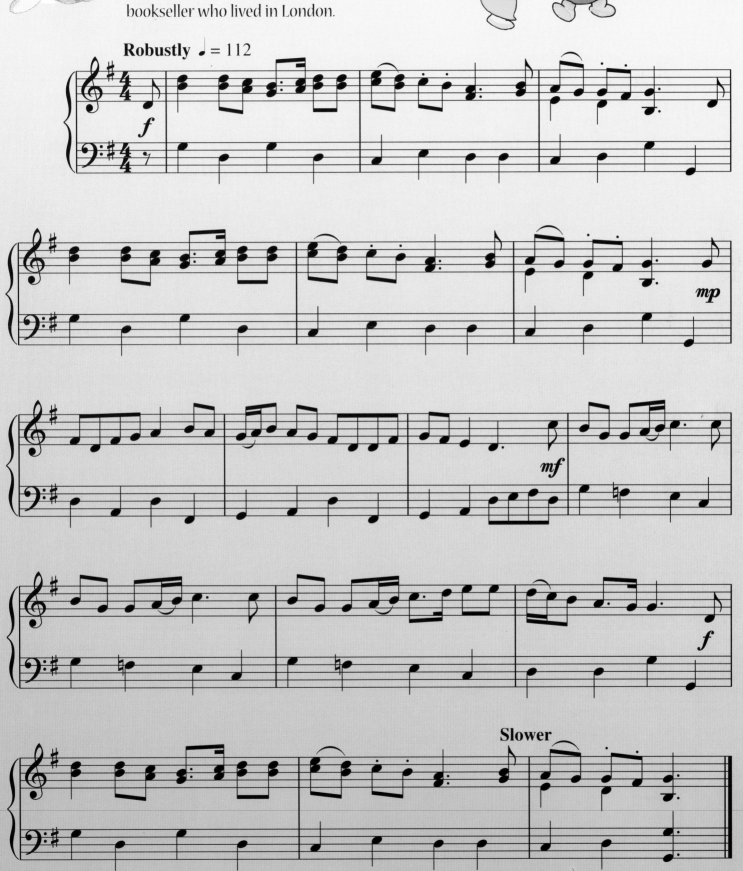

Two by two

This tune is also called "When Johnny comes marching home". It was written by Patrick Gilmore, an American bandmaster, in the 1860s.

Three into two

This tune was written specially for this book. There are five beats in each bar. Count three, then two.

Thoughtfully ♩ = 96

17

Ma Normandie

A French songwriter, Frédéric Bérat, wrote
this tune in 1836. Bérat was born in Rouen,
a city in Normandy. Normandy is famous
for its butter, milk and cheese.

Les trois rois

"Les trois rois" is a very old Christmas song from Provence in the south of France. The title means "The three kings". Play this like a march, with a very crisp rhythm.

You could imitate the sound of an old French marching band by asking someone to play the tune on the recorder. Someone else could beat a drum. Use the rhythm in the left hand of the first two bars of the third line.

Oh happy day!

This is an old song, but it was made famous in the 1960s by the Edwin Hawkins Singers, an American Gospel choir.

Swing low, sweet chariot

This tune was first written down around 1915
by Harry Thacker Burleigh, a composer whose
grandfather was a slave in the southern USA.

Star of the County Down

County Down is in Northern Ireland. This ancient Irish tune was first published in 1726. It is also known as "Gilderoy".

Ask someone to play this tune with you on the flute or violin. (You could copy it out to make it easier to read.) Before you begin, count a few bars so that you all start together.

Or use this easier part. Wait two bars for the piano introduction, then play the music below eight times on recorder, flute, chime bars or violin.

Galway city

Galway is a city in the west of Ireland.
This tune was first published in 1624.
It is also known as "Spanish ladies".

O sole mio

Two Italian men, Eduardo Di Capua and
Giovanni Capurro, wrote this in Naples in 1896.
The title means "My sunshine".